FEMINISM, AI, BIG TECH, AND SOCIETAL ISSUES

Navigating the Nexus

Sarnia de la Mare

Tale Teller Club Publishing

CONTENTS

FEMINISM, AI, BIG TECH, AND SOCIETAL ISSUES: NAVIGATING THE NEXUS

In the digital age, where algorithms shape our lives and technology permeates every facet of society, the convergence of feminism, AI, and big tech has become both inevitable and consequential. These seemingly disparate realms intersect in profound ways, influencing not only how we interact with technology but also the very fabric of our social structures.

The Gendered Algorithms

Behind every recommendation, search result, and personalized ad lies an algorithm—a mathematical construct designed to optimize outcomes. However, these algorithms are not neutral. They inherit biases from their creators and the data they learn from. When it comes to gender, these biases can perpetuate stereotypes, reinforce inequalities, and exclude marginalized voices.

Feminist scholars and activists have raised alarm bells about the gendered impact of AI. From biased hiring algorithms to discriminatory credit scoring models, technology can inadvertently amplify existing disparities. Understanding and rectifying these biases is essential for building a more equitable digital landscape.

Representation Matters

Diversity within the tech industry remains a pressing issue. Women, especially those from underrepresented backgrounds, continue to face barriers in accessing tech education, entering STEM fields, and ascending the corporate ladder. Without diverse perspectives shaping AI development, we risk creating systems that fail to serve everyone.

Feminism calls for representation—not just in user interfaces but also in boardrooms, research labs, and coding communities. When women and non-binary individuals actively participate in shaping AI, we move closer to technology that reflects the needs and aspirations of all.

Ethical Dilemmas

Big tech companies wield immense power. Their decisions impact privacy, democracy, and social cohesion. Feminist ethics demand that we scrutinize this power. Are AI-driven surveillance systems disproportionately targeting women? How do algorithms perpetuate harmful beauty standards? Can we ensure consent in data collection?

As we navigate these ethical dilemmas, feminist perspectives offer a compass. They remind us to prioritize human well-being over profit, challenge the status quo, and center empathy in technological design.

Tech Activism and Solidarity

Feminism and tech activism converge in grassroots movements. From #MeToo to campaigns against online harassment, women have harnessed digital platforms to amplify their voices. These movements intersect with AI ethics, demanding accountability from tech giants and advocating for transparency.

Solidarity across disciplines—feminism, AI research, policy, and activism—is essential. Together, we can envision a future where technology serves humanity rather than perpetuating its biases.

This introduction merely scratches the surface of a complex and evolving landscape. As we delve deeper, we must recognize that feminism isn't just about gender—it's about dismantling power imbalances, fostering inclusion, and shaping a world where technology uplifts us all.

THE GENDERED ALGORITHM

Gendered algorithms, often unintentionally biased, can perpetuate gender stereotypes and inequalities.

Here are **some examples**:

Consumer Credit Algorithms:

> In the consumer credit industry, AI systems determine creditworthiness based on historical data. Unfortunately, these systems often learn from patterns where women receive **lower credit limits** than men, even with similar financial profiles.
> For instance, a woman with the same income, expenses, and debt as her husband might receive a significantly lower credit limit.

Facial Analysis Systems:

> Some facial analysis tools use a **gender binary** (male/female) for classification. However, this simplistic view fails to account for non-binary or diverse gender identities, reinforcing stereotypes.
> These inaccuracies affect not only gender representation but also the well-being of women and non-binary individuals.

Job Role Bias in Search Engine Ads:

> Search engine ad algorithms can inadvertently reinforce **gender bias** in job roles. Certain ads may be shown

more frequently to specific genders, perpetuating existing inequalities.

Generative AI Art Generation:

Academic research found bias in generative AI art applications. When asked to create images of people in specialized professions, the system consistently depicted older people as men, reinforcing gendered biases about women's roles in the workplace.

Hiring Algorithms:

Amazon discontinued a hiring algorithm that favored applicants based on certain words (e.g., "executed" or "captured") commonly found on men's resumes. This highlights how algorithms can inadvertently perpetuate gender disparities.

Healthcare Algorithms:

AI systems in healthcare may prioritize certain patients for COVID-19 vaccines. If these systems are trained on biased data, they might inadvertently disadvantage women or other marginalized groups.

Educational Algorithms:

Algorithms used in education can impact opportunities for students. If they reinforce gender stereotypes or fail to address diverse needs, they perpetuate inequality.

Remember that addressing gender bias in algorithms requires vigilance, diverse representation in AI development, and ongoing scrutiny to create more equitable systems.

How might professionals use AI to support the integration of feminist theory into gender education?

AI can play a significant role in identifying potentially vulnerable women and girls. Here are some ways it can assist professionals:

Data Analysis and Pattern Recognition:

> AI algorithms can analyze large datasets to identify patterns associated with vulnerability. By examining factors such as age, socioeconomic status, education, and living conditions, AI can flag individuals who may be at risk.

> For example, machine learning models can predict vulnerability based on historical data and risk factors.

Natural Language Processing (NLP):

> NLP techniques allow AI to process and understand text. Professionals can use AI-powered chatbots or sentiment analysis tools to assess the emotional state of women and girls.
> Detecting distress signals in online communication (such as social media posts or chat messages) can help identify those in need.

Behavioral Analysis:

> AI can analyze behavioral patterns to detect signs of vulnerability. For instance:
>> Unusual spending patterns (indicating financial distress)
>> Changes in communication frequency or social

interactions
Frequent searches related to mental health or abuse

Professionals can use this information to intervene early.

Image and Video Analysis:

AI can analyze images and videos to identify signs of vulnerability or distress. For instance:
Facial expressions (sadness, fear, anxiety)
Bruises or physical harm
Unsafe environments (e.g., cluttered or chaotic spaces)

Professionals can use image recognition models to flag concerning content.

Predictive Models:

AI can build predictive models based on historical data. These models can estimate the likelihood of vulnerability based on various factors.
For example, predicting which girls are at risk of dropping out of school or becoming victims of child marriage.

Early Warning Systems:

AI-powered systems can provide alerts when specific risk factors are detected. These systems can be integrated into social services, schools, or healthcare settings.
Professionals can receive notifications about vulnerable individuals, allowing for timely intervention.

Privacy-Preserving Techniques:

AI can respect privacy while identifying vulnerability. Techniques like federated learning or differential privacy allow models to learn from distributed data without exposing personal information.

Professionals can work with anonymized data to protect

individuals 'privacy.

Collaboration with Human Experts:

> AI should complement, not replace, human expertise. Professionals can collaborate with AI tools to make informed decisions.

> Combining AI insights with social workers 'assessments ensures a holistic approach.

Remember that while AI can assist, ethical considerations, privacy, and cultural context are crucial.

Professionals must use AI tools responsibly and in conjunction with their expertise to support vulnerable women and girls.

CHALLENGES OF USING AI IN IDENTIFYING VULNERABLE WOMEN AND GIRLS

Identifying vulnerable women and girls using AI presents several challenges:

Bias and Fairness:

AI models can inherit biases from training data. If historical data reflects societal biases, the AI may perpetuate them.
Vulnerable groups, including women and girls, may be underrepresented in training data, leading to biased predictions.

Privacy Concerns:

Balancing the need for accurate identification with privacy protection is challenging.
AI systems must handle sensitive information carefully to avoid harm or breaches.

Contextual Complexity:

Vulnerability is context-dependent. AI models struggle to

capture nuanced situations.
Factors like cultural norms, family dynamics, and individual experiences impact vulnerability.

Dynamic Nature of Vulnerability:

Vulnerability changes over time. AI models need to adapt to evolving circumstances.
Static models may miss emerging risks.

Lack of Ground Truth Labels:

Identifying vulnerability often lacks clear labels. What defines a "vulnerable" person varies.
Supervised learning relies on labeled data, which may not exist for all cases.

Intersectionality:

Vulnerability intersects with race, ethnicity, disability, and other identities.
AI must consider these intersections to avoid oversimplification.

Resource Constraints:

Implementing AI solutions requires resources (computing power, data, expertise).
Many organizations lack these resources, especially in low-resource settings.

Ethical Dilemmas:

AI decisions impact lives. Balancing accuracy with ethical considerations is crucial.
False positives (labeling someone vulnerable incorrectly) and false negatives (missing actual vulnerability) have real consequences.

Transparency and Explainability:

AI models often lack transparency. Understanding how they arrive at decisions is essential.
Explainable AI methods are crucial for building trust.

Human-AI Collaboration:

AI should complement human judgment, not replace it.
Professionals need training to interpret AI outputs effectively.

In summary, while AI offers promise, addressing these challenges requires interdisciplinary collaboration, ethical guidelines, and ongoing research.

ADDRESSING THE ISSUE OF BIAS IN AI

Addressing bias in AI is critical to ensure equitable and fair outcomes.

Here are some strategies:

Diverse and Representative Data:

> Collect diverse data: Ensure that training data includes a wide range of demographics, backgrounds, and perspectives.
>
> Avoid underrepresentation: Pay attention to minority groups and avoid skewed representation.

Bias Detection and Mitigation:

> Audit models: Regularly assess AI models for bias. Use tools to detect and quantify bias.
> Mitigate bias: Adjust algorithms to reduce disparities. Techniques include reweighting data, modifying loss functions, and adversarial training.

Fairness Metrics:

> Define fairness metrics: Quantify fairness (e.g., demographic parity, equalized odds).
> Monitor models using these metrics during development and deployment.

Explainable AI (XAI):

Interpretability: Make AI decisions transparent. Use techniques like LIME, SHAP, or attention maps.

Model explanations: Explain why a model made a specific prediction.

Regularization Techniques:

L1 and L2 regularization: Penalize extreme model weights. Fairness-aware regularization: Incorporate fairness constraints during training.

Preprocessing and Postprocessing:

Preprocessing: Remove sensitive attributes (e.g., gender, race) from data.
Postprocessing: Adjust model outputs to achieve fairness.

Contextual Fairness:

Consider context: Fairness depends on the specific use case and context.
Avoid one-size-fits-all approaches.

Human-in-the-Loop:

Involve human experts: They can identify and address bias.
Use AI as an aid, not a replacement.

Ethical Guidelines and Policies:

Develop clear guidelines: Organizations should have policies on bias, fairness, and ethical AI.
Regularly review and update these guidelines.

Education and Awareness:

Train AI practitioners: Raise awareness about bias and its impact.
Foster a culture of responsible AI development.

Remember, addressing bias is an ongoing process. Collaboration, transparency, and commitment are essential to building fair AI systems.

How we might use feminist theory and AI in the education of young adults to understand and limit misogyny.

Feminist theory and AI intersect in powerful ways, especially when it comes to educating young adults about misogyny.

Let's explore how they can be useful:

Feminist AI: Critical Perspectives:

> Feminist AI brings feminist theory, knowledge, and methods to analyze how AI impacts social justice and inequality.
> By integrating feminist insights, educators can help young adults understand the gendered implications of AI systems.

Challenging Gender Bias in AI:

> Feminist theory encourages critical examination of biases. AI often reflects societal biases, including misogyny.
> Educators can teach young adults to recognize and question gender bias in AI algorithms and applications.

Representation and Diversity:

> Feminist AI emphasizes diverse representation. Educators can discuss the lack of women and minorities in AI development.
> Young adults learn that diverse perspectives lead to more equitable AI.

Ethical AI Design:
> Feminist theory promotes ethical considerations. Educators can discuss the ethical dimensions of AI, including privacy,

consent, and fairness.
Young adults can engage in discussions about responsible AI design.

Gendered Effects of AI:

Feminist AI examines how AI impacts different genders. Educators can explore how AI systems may perpetuate harmful stereotypes or reinforce misogyny.
Young adults learn to critically assess AI technologies.

Data and Bias:

Feminist theory highlights data biases. Educators can discuss how biased data affect AI outcomes.
Young adults can explore ways to mitigate bias during AI development.

Intersectionality and AI:

Feminist theory considers intersectionality (race, class, sexuality). Educators can discuss how these intersect with AI impacts.
Young adults learn that AI affects people differently based on multiple identities.

Feminist Movements and Data:

Feminist AI examines data use. Educators can discuss how feminist movements leverage data for advocacy.
Young adults explore how data can drive social change.

Queer Technological Futures:

Feminist theory encourages envisioning alternative futures. Educators can discuss queer and feminist perspectives on technology.
Young adults engage in imagining more inclusive AI futures.

Structural Dynamics of AI:

Feminist AI goes beyond individual liability. Educators can explore broader systemic issues related to AI.
Young adults learn to consider AI's societal impact.

In summary, integrating feminist theory and AI education empowers young adults to critically engage with technology, challenge biases, and work toward a more just and equitable world.

Here are some examples of feminist AI research that explore the intersection of gender, technology, and artificial intelligence:

Feminist AI Publications:
The Feminist AI initiative by the <A+> Alliance focuses on creating algorithmic decision-making systems and AI designed with inclusion at the core.

Feminist Data Set:
An art project that investigates and critiques machine learning through an intersectional feminist lens.

Rethinking AI through Feminism:

Researchers explore how Feminist AI can be shaped in various ways:

As a model
In design
Through policy
As part of culture
In discourse
As a scientific field3.

Practicing Feminist Principles in AI Design:

Examines how AI can challenge social inequality and dismantle power structures.

Integrates feminist principles into AI development1.

Feminist Data Collection:

Explores building an inclusive system through feminist data collection.

Recommendations and examples for implementing data feminism principles are discussed1.

Data against Feminicide:

Investigates the role of data in understanding and addressing feminicide (gender-based killings of women).

Highlights the importance of collecting and using the right data to tackle this issue1.

Debiasing the Algorithm:

Explores ethics, definitions, and metrics related to fairness in AI.

Discusses how real-world deployment and usage of models matter as much as their design1.

What is Fairness?:

Reflects on efforts to debias data and create fair machine learning models.

Raises questions about defining and achieving fairness in AI1.

A View from Another Set of Eyes:

Considers algorithms as instructions that process data to generate outputs.

Examines how AI shapes our understanding of the world and its biases1.

These examples demonstrate how feminist perspectives enrich AI research, promote fairness, and challenge existing norms. By integrating feminist theory, we can create more equitable and socially responsible AI systems.

HOW CAN FEMINIST AI BE APPLIED TO SOCIAL JUSTICE ISSUES?

Feminist AI can significantly impact social justice issues by challenging biases, promoting equity, and fostering inclusivity. Here are some ways it can be applied:

Gender Bias Detection:

> Feminist AI can analyze algorithms, data, and systems to identify gender bias.
> By flagging biased outcomes, it helps rectify discriminatory practices in areas like hiring, lending, and criminal justice.

Fairness in AI Decision-Making:

> Feminist AI advocates for fairness. It ensures that AI systems do not disproportionately harm marginalized groups.
> By designing fair algorithms, we reduce disparities and promote social justice.

Healthcare Equity:

> Feminist AI can address gender bias in healthcare. It ensures that medical algorithms consider diverse patient populations.
> By accounting for intersectionality (race, sexuality, disability), it improves health outcomes for all.

Gender-Based Violence Prevention:

Feminist AI aids in identifying patterns of violence against women and girls.
It can predict risk factors, support early intervention, and empower survivors.

Inclusive Language Models:

Feminist AI contributes to language models that avoid harmful stereotypes.
It promotes respectful and inclusive language, reducing bias in communication.

Representation in Tech:

Feminist AI encourages diverse representation in AI development.
By including more women, non-binary individuals, and underrepresented groups, we create better technologies.

Ethical Data Collection:

Feminist AI emphasizes ethical data practices.
It ensures that data collection respects privacy, consent, and cultural context.

Education and Awareness:

Feminist AI educates practitioners and the public about AI's impact.
By raising awareness, it fosters critical thinking and responsible AI use.

Policy Advocacy:

Feminist AI engages in policy discussions.
It advocates for regulations that promote fairness, transparency, and accountability.

AI for Social Good:

Feminist AI aligns with broader efforts for social justice.

It contributes to a more equitable world by challenging norms and biases.

In summary, Feminist AI is a powerful tool for advancing social justice, dismantling discrimination, and creating a more inclusive technological landscape.

HOW CAN WE ENSURE THAT FEMINIST AI IS INCLUSIVE AND EQUITABLE?

Ensuring that feminist AI is inclusive and equitable involves intentional efforts and considerations.

Here are some key steps:

Diverse Representation in AI Development:

> Include diverse voices: Ensure that women, non-binary individuals, and underrepresented groups actively participate in AI research and development.
>
> Intersectionality: Recognize that identities intersect (race, sexuality, disability). Consider these intersections in AI design.

Ethical Data Collection and Labeling:

> Collect diverse data: Ensure that training data represent various demographics and experiences.
>
> Avoid biased labeling: Be cautious when labeling data to prevent reinforcing stereotypes.

Bias Detection and Mitigation:

Audit AI models: Regularly assess for bias. Use tools to detect and quantify disparities.
Mitigate bias: Adjust algorithms to reduce unfair outcomes.

Fairness Metrics and Evaluation:

Define fairness metrics: Quantify fairness (e.g., demographic parity, equalized odds).
Continuously evaluate models using these metrics during development and deployment.

Transparency and Explainability:

Make AI decisions transparent: Explain how models arrive at conclusions.
Use techniques like LIME, SHAP, or attention maps to enhance interpretability.

Contextual Understanding:

Recognize that fairness depends on context. What's fair in one situation may not be in another.
Avoid one-size-fits-all approaches.

Human-in-the-Loop Approach:

Involve human experts: They can identify and address bias.
Use AI as an aid, not a replacement.

Education and Awareness:

Train AI practitioners: Raise awareness about bias, fairness, and ethical considerations.
Foster a culture of responsible AI development.

Policy and Regulation:

Advocate for policies that promote fairness and equity in AI.
Encourage transparency, accountability, and ethical guidelines.

Collaboration and Accountability:

> Work together: Researchers, policymakers, and practitioners must collaborate.
> Hold organizations accountable for addressing bias and promoting inclusivity.

Remember that creating inclusive and equitable AI requires ongoing commitment and vigilance. By integrating feminist principles, we can build AI systems that benefit everyone.

WHAT ARE SOME CHALLENGES OF IMPLEMENTING FEMINIST AI IN PRACTICE?

Implementing feminist AI in practice comes with several challenges:

Biased Data:

> Challenge: Existing data often reflects societal biases, including gender bias. Biased data can perpetuate inequalities.
> Mitigation: Collect diverse and representative data. Be aware of underrepresentation and actively address bias during data collection.

Algorithmic Bias:

> Challenge: AI models can inherit biases from training data. These biases may lead to discriminatory outcomes.
> Mitigation: Regularly audit models for bias. Adjust algorithms to reduce disparities. Define fairness metrics and evaluate models accordingly.

Intersectionality Complexity:

Challenge: Vulnerability is multifaceted, intersecting with race, class, sexuality, and disability. AI must consider these intersections.

Mitigation: Avoid oversimplification. Understand that vulnerability is context-dependent and varies across identities.

Privacy and Consent:

Challenge: AI systems often process personal data. Balancing accurate identification with privacy protection is crucial.

Mitigation: Handle sensitive information carefully. Use anonymization techniques and respect consent.

Ethical Dilemmas:

Challenge: AI decisions impact lives. Balancing accuracy with ethical considerations is complex.

Mitigation: Consider the consequences of false positives and false negatives. Prioritize ethical guidelines.

Resource Constraints:

Challenge: Implementing AI solutions requires resources (computing power, data, expertise).

Mitigation: Advocate for resource allocation. Collaborate with organizations and policymakers.

Human-AI Collaboration:

Challenge: AI should complement human judgment, not replace it.

Mitigation: Involve human experts. Use AI as an aid, guided by human insights.

Cultural Context:

Challenge: AI operates in diverse cultural contexts. What's

fair or inclusive varies across societies.

Mitigation: Adapt AI approaches to specific cultural norms and values.

Education and Awareness:

Challenge: Raising awareness about feminist AI is essential.

Mitigation: Train practitioners, policymakers, and the public. Foster a culture of responsible AI development.

Policy and Regulation:

Challenge: Lack of clear guidelines and policies for feminist AI.

Mitigation: Advocate for regulations that promote fairness, transparency, and accountability.

In summary, addressing these challenges requires interdisciplinary collaboration, ethical guidelines, and ongoing research to create more equitable AI systems.

Using AI to create a better understanding of feminism for young people who reject its basic principles

Feminist AI offers a unique opportunity to engage young people who may initially reject feminist principles. Here's how it can foster understanding:

Interactive Chatbots and Conversations:

> Feminist chatbots can engage in conversations with young people.
> By addressing misconceptions, answering questions, and providing context, chatbots can gradually shift perspectives.

Education Through Examples:

> AI systems can analyze historical examples of gender inequality and feminist movements.
> By presenting facts and stories, AI can illustrate the importance of feminism in addressing societal issues.

Exploring Intersectionality:

> Feminist AI can introduce the concept of intersectionality (how gender intersects with race, class, sexuality, etc.).
> Young people learn that feminism is not one-size-fits-all but considers diverse experiences.

Media Analysis:

> AI algorithms can analyze media content (films,

advertisements, news) for gender bias.
By revealing hidden stereotypes, AI encourages critical thinking about media messages.

Ethical AI Design Challenges:

Feminist AI prompts discussions about ethical design.
Young people explore how AI reflects societal values and biases.

Inclusive Language Models:

AI language models can be trained to use inclusive language.
By avoiding gender stereotypes, AI models promote respectful communication.

Interactive Workshops and Tools:

Practical tools can guide young people through discussions.
Workshops on bias, fairness, and ethics encourage active participation.

Representation in Tech:

Feminist AI emphasizes diverse representation in AI development.
Young people learn that technology should reflect everyone's needs.

Critical Reflection:

AI systems can prompt self-reflection.
By asking questions about biases and assumptions, AI encourages introspection.

Collaboration with Educators:

Feminist AI collaborates with educators to create age-appropriate content.
By integrating feminist principles into curricula, we reach young minds effectively.

In summary, Feminist AI bridges the gap by engaging young people, challenging stereotypes, and promoting critical thinking about gender equality.

Using technologies for safety in interrelation situations

Feminist perspectives can significantly enhance technologies designed for safety in interpersonal situations. Let's explore how:
Shift from Security to Safety:

> Challenge: Traditionally, technology focuses on security (protecting against external threats). However, safety encompasses a broader context, including well-being, freedom from harm, and self-determination.
>
> Feminist Approach: By using feminist epistemologies, we shift the paradigm from security to safety. This means considering the safety needs of diverse user groups beyond conventional threat models.

Holistic Safety Considerations:

> Challenge: Some technologies inadvertently generate different safety experiences for different user groups.
>
> Feminist Approach: We advocate for holistic safety. This involves understanding safety as highly contextual, subject to ethical and political dimensions. Safety should be grounded in justice and consider the needs of all individuals.

Trust and Abusability Concepts:

> Trust: Reimagining trust in technology means considering whose trust matters and how it is built. Trust should not perpetuate existing power imbalances.
>
> Abusability: We must anticipate how technologies can be misused or abused. A feminist lens helps us design systems that minimize harm.

Complexity of Safety Work:

Challenge: Some individuals perform "safety work" – mental and physical labor to keep themselves safe. This work varies based on context, person, and time.

Feminist Approach: We recognize this complexity and aim to build technologies that alleviate safety work rather than burden users.

Appealing to Greater Inclusion:

Challenge: Safety discussions should prioritize marginalized groups. We need to question whose safety is prioritized and how inclusion can be improved.

Feminist Approach: By shifting the conversation from security to safety, we encourage critical questions about inclusion and advocate for meaningful protection.

THE SUITABILITY OF APPS, COULD THEY BE USEFUL?

Health Monitoring and Alerts:

App Functionality: Develop an app that monitors health parameters (such as heart rate, blood pressure, and temperature) using wearable devices or sensors.

AI Component: Implement AI algorithms to detect anomalies or health deterioration. Send real-time alerts to caregivers or emergency services when needed.

Fall Detection and Assistance:

App Functionality: Create an app that detects falls using smartphone sensors or wearables.

AI Component: Train AI models to recognize fall patterns. When a fall occurs, the app can automatically call for help or notify caregivers.

Medication Reminders and Management:

App Functionality: Design an app that reminds users to take medications on time.

AI Component: Use AI to personalize reminders based on individual schedules and medication requirements.

Virtual Assistants for Daily Tasks:

App Functionality: Integrate a virtual assistant (like a

chatbot) within the app.

AI Component: Train the assistant to handle common queries, set reminders, and provide information about daily tasks.

Emotional Support and Mental Health:

App Functionality: Include features for emotional support, meditation, or relaxation exercises.

AI Component: Develop AI chatbots that engage in empathetic conversations, offer coping strategies, and connect users to mental health resources.

Navigation and Wayfinding:

App Functionality: Create a navigation tool for indoor spaces (e.g., hospitals, offices, or homes).

AI Component: Use AI to improve indoor positioning accuracy, especially for visually impaired individuals.

Workplace Accommodations:

App Functionality: Customize workplace settings based on individual needs (e.g., font size, screen brightness, or noise reduction).

AI Component: Adapt settings dynamically using AI algorithms that learn from user preferences.

Emergency Response and Panic Buttons:

App Functionality: Include an emergency button that triggers immediate assistance.

AI Component: Optimize response times by using AI to route emergency calls to the nearest responders.

Financial Management and Budgeting:

App Functionality: Assist vulnerable individuals in managing finances, paying bills, and tracking expenses.

AI Component: Predict future expenses, provide budgeting

tips, and identify potential financial risks.

Job Matching and Skill Development:

> App Functionality: Help vulnerable job seekers find suitable employment opportunities.
> AI Component: Use AI to match skills, preferences, and qualifications with available job listings.

Remember that user-centered design, privacy considerations, and ongoing feedback from vulnerable individuals are essential for successful implementation. By combining app functionality with AI capabilities, we can create powerful tools that enhance the well-being and independence of vulnerable populations.

Here are some examples of feminist technologies designed to enhance safety:

Panic Button Apps:

> Functionality: These apps turn smartphones into secret alarms that can be activated in emergencies.
> AI Component: They can alert a user's network or emergency services when needed.

Feminist Chatbots for Emotional Support:

> Functionality: Chatbots engage in empathetic conversations, offer coping strategies, and connect users to mental health resources.
> AI Component: These chatbots use natural language processing to provide emotional support.

Inclusive Navigation Tools:

> Functionality: Indoor navigation apps for spaces like hospitals or offices.
> AI Component: AI improves indoor positioning accuracy, especially for visually impaired individuals.

Gender-Inclusive Language Models:

Functionality: Language models that avoid harmful stereotypes and promote respectful communication.

AI Component: AI is trained to use inclusive language.

Community Networks for Safety:

Functionality: Community-based networks that provide connectivity and safety.

AI Component: AI can optimize network deployment and ensure equitable access.

Personalized Safety Reminders:

Functionality: Apps that remind users to take safety precautions (e.g., locking doors, checking surroundings).

AI Component: AI personalizes reminders based on individual contexts and routines.

Emergency Response Systems:

Functionality: Apps with panic buttons that trigger immediate assistance.

AI Component: Optimize response times by using AI to route emergency calls to nearby responders.

Privacy-Enhancing Tools:

Functionality: Apps that protect user privacy (e.g., secure messaging, encrypted calls).

AI Component: AI can identify potential privacy risks and recommend protective measures.

Workplace Safety Apps:

Functionality: Apps that address workplace safety concerns (e.g., reporting harassment, unsafe conditions).

AI Component: AI can analyze workplace data to identify patterns and risks.

Safety Auditing Tools:

Functionality: Apps that assess physical spaces for safety

(e.g., well-lit areas, emergency exits).
AI Component: AI can automate safety audits and recommend improvements.

Remember that feminist technologies prioritize inclusion, equity, and the well-being of all users, especially vulnerable populations.

In conclusion, **feminist approaches to AI** play a pivotal role in addressing domestic abuse. By integrating feminist principles into AI systems, we can create more effective and compassionate solutions:

Understanding Intersectionality:

Feminist AI recognizes that domestic abuse affects individuals differently based on their intersecting identities (gender, race, class, sexuality, disability).
It ensures that AI responses consider these complexities and avoid one-size-fits-all approaches.

Challenging Gender Bias:

Feminist AI actively questions and mitigates gender bias in algorithms.
It promotes fair treatment and equitable outcomes for survivors of domestic abuse.

Empowering Survivors:

Feminist AI provides tools for survivors to seek help, access resources, and connect with support networks.
It prioritizes user agency and autonomy.

Privacy and Safety:

Feminist AI designs systems that protect survivors 'privacy and safety.
It avoids retraumatization and ensures that technology does

not inadvertently harm those seeking assistance.

Trauma-Informed Design:

Feminist AI considers the emotional and psychological impact of technology on survivors.
It avoids triggering traumatic memories and fosters a sense of control.

Community Building and Solidarity:

Feminist AI connects survivors to online communities, helplines, and local services.
It fosters solidarity and collective support.

Ethical Data Collection:

Feminist AI collects data ethically, respecting survivors' consent and confidentiality.
It avoids perpetuating harmful stereotypes.

Collaboration with Advocates and Experts:

Feminist AI collaborates with domestic violence experts, social workers, and survivors.
It ensures that technology aligns with real-world needs.

In the fight against domestic abuse, feminist AI serves as a powerful ally, amplifying survivor voices, challenging norms, and contributing to a safer and more compassionate world .

HOW MIGHT SOCIETY ENCOURAGE BIG TECH TO FINANCE MORE GENDER EGALITARIANISM IN NEW PRODUCTS?

Gender equality is a crucial goal, and encouraging big tech companies to finance more gender-egalitarian products can lead to positive change. Here are some strategies that society can consider:

Tailoring Financial Products: Big tech companies can design and offer financial products that specifically meet the needs of women. This could include personalized investment platforms, savings accounts, or credit options that address gender-specific challenges.

Promoting Gender-Inclusive Technologies: Encouraging the development of technologies that empower women and girls is essential. These technologies should provide equal access to education, healthcare, and financial services. For instance, creating user-friendly apps for financial literacy or entrepreneurship can help bridge gender gaps.

Increasing Representation: Big tech companies should actively promote gender diversity within their workforce. By hiring and retaining more women in leadership positions, these companies can influence product development and decision-making processes. Diverse perspectives lead to more inclusive products.

Raising Awareness: Society can advocate for gender equality by raising awareness about the importance of financing gender-egalitarian products. This includes educating consumers, investors, and policymakers about the impact of such initiatives.

Collaboration and Partnerships: Big tech companies can collaborate with organizations, NGOs, and governments to create joint initiatives. These partnerships can fund research, innovation, and projects that advance gender equality in technology and finance.

Progress toward gender equality requires collective effort. By encouraging big tech to invest in gender-egalitarian products, we can create a more inclusive and equitable future for all.

Realistically, venture capitalists can indeed find profits in feminist-friendly software.

Market Demand: There is a growing demand for software and products that align with feminist values. Consumers are increasingly conscious of gender equality, diversity, and social impact. Investing in software that caters to this demand can lead to a loyal customer base and sustainable revenue

Untapped Markets: Feminist-friendly software can address underserved markets. For instance:

Healthcare: Apps that focus on women's health, reproductive rights, and mental well-being.

Financial Inclusion: Platforms that empower women economically, such as budgeting tools, investment apps, or microfinance platforms.

Education: E-learning platforms that promote gender equality and provide accessible education for all.

Corporate Social Responsibility (CSR): Many companies prioritize CSR initiatives. Investing in feminist-friendly software aligns with their commitment to social impact. It enhances brand reputation and attracts socially conscious investors and customers.

Innovation: Software that challenges gender stereotypes and promotes inclusivity can drive innovation. Think of apps that combat workplace bias, encourage diversity, or facilitate networking for women entrepreneurs. These innovations can lead to competitive advantages and profits.

Long-Term Vision: Venture capitalists who recognize the long-term benefits of gender equality invest in software that contributes to positive societal change. While immediate profits may vary, the long-term impact can be substantial.

In summary, venture capitalists can see profits by investing in feminist-friendly software, provided they understand the market dynamics, social impact, and the evolving needs of diverse users.

HOW MIGHT WE MEASURE THE FINANCIAL SUCCESS OR FAILURE OF GENDER EQUALITY MOTIVATED SOFTWARE?

Measuring the impact of gender equality initiatives, including feminist-friendly software, is essential to assess their effectiveness and guide future efforts. Here are some ways to measure impact:

Quantitative Metrics:

> **User Adoption**: Track the number of users, downloads, or active participants using the software. High adoption rates indicate relevance and acceptance.

> **Engagement**: Measure user engagement, such as time spent on the platform, frequency of use, and interactions. Active engagement signifies value.

> **Conversion Rates**: Evaluate how many users take desired

actions (e.g., signing up, making purchases). Higher conversion rates indicate successful impact.

Financial Metrics: Assess revenue generated directly from the software. This includes subscriptions, in-app purchases, or ad revenue.

Market Share: Compare the software's market share with competitors. A growing share suggests impact.

Qualitative Assessment:

User Feedback: Collect feedback through surveys, reviews, or focus groups. Understand user experiences, satisfaction, and perceived impact.

Case Studies: Conduct in-depth case studies with users. Explore how the software positively affects their lives, behaviors, or attitudes.

Testimonials: Gather testimonials from users who benefited from the software. These personal stories demonstrate impact.

Stakeholder Interviews: Interview stakeholders (developers, investors, users) to understand their perspectives on impact.

Social Media Sentiment: Analyze social media conversations related to the software. Positive sentiment indicates impact.

Social Impact Indicators:

Gender Equality Index: Use existing indices or create custom ones to measure gender equality within the software's ecosystem.

Access and Inclusion: Assess whether the software reaches marginalized groups, including women from diverse backgrounds.

Empowerment: Evaluate whether the software empowers women economically, socially, or educationally.

Behavioral Change: Monitor changes in user behavior related to gender norms, stereotypes, or biases.

Long-Term Effects:

Societal Change: Consider the broader impact beyond immediate metrics. Does the software contribute to changing societal norms or policies?

Economic Empowerment: Measure the software's role in women's economic independence, financial literacy, and entrepreneurship.

Educational Impact: Assess whether the software enhances education, skills, and career opportunities for women.

Comparative Analysis:

Benchmarking: Compare the software's impact against similar initiatives or industry standards.

Before-and-After Analysis: Evaluate impact by comparing data before and after implementing the software.

Remember that impact measurement is multifaceted. A combination of quantitative and qualitative methods provides a comprehensive view of how feminist-friendly software influences individuals, communities, and society as a whole.

CONCLUSION:

In the intricate web of technology, gender dynamics, and societal impact, the convergence of feminism, AI, and big tech holds both promise and peril.

Gendered Algorithms: Beneath the sleek interfaces lie algorithms that encode biases. These digital decision-makers perpetuate stereotypes, affecting credit scores, job opportunities, and even healthcare access. Recognizing these biases is the first step toward dismantling them.

Representation Matters: The tech industry remains a male-dominated realm. Yet, diversity fuels innovation. When women and non-binary individuals actively shape AI, we break free from the echo chambers of binary thinking. Representation isn't just about headcounts; it's about amplifying diverse voices.

Ethical Dilemmas: Big tech wields immense power. As algorithms influence our lives, we grapple with ethical questions. How do we balance profit with social responsibility? Can we ensure consent in data collection? Feminist ethics remind us to prioritize humanity over algorithms.

Tech Activism and Solidarity: From #MeToo to digital rights campaigns, women have harnessed technology to reclaim agency. These movements intersect with AI ethics, demanding transparency, accountability, and justice.

Solidarity across disciplines—feminism, AI research, and activism—fuels collective vision.

Feminism isn't an add-on; it's the very fabric of ethical tech. Let our code be infused with empathy, our data sets diverse, and our algorithms instruments of liberation.